How to have a
GREAT DAY EVERYDAY!

**By
STEVE BECK**

A Gift to

_____

From

_____

Published by Beck & Associates

Library of Congress Cataloging-in-Publication Data
Beck, Steve, 1953-
How To Have A Great Day Everyday
by Steve Beck   p.cm.

ISBN 0-9754817-9-7
1 Conduct of Life.   I. Title
BJ1581.2.B39 2006, 158.1 – dc22
          2006011928

"The Paradoxical Commandments" reprinted with the permission of the author. Copyright Kent M. Keith 1968, renewed 2001. www.paradoxicalcommandments.com

Printed in the United States of America

Fourth Printing 11/2013

Table of Contents

Foreword

Steve Beck is known around the nation as an energetic communicator and coach. Through his numerous seminars, workshops, and speaking engagements he has taught thousands "How To Have A Great Day Everyday."

The book you hold is simple, yet intelligent. Steve's message helps us all realize that we are in control of our thoughts, emotions, and our interactions with others. He teaches us to look beyond our problems and see possibilities.

We are all brought into this world with special gifts. Steve helps us discover what those gifts are and motivates us to work on sharing them with others.

I have had the privilege of working with Steve over many years. He lives the principles in this book. What he is suggesting to you, he does.

Recently, I asked Steve at what age he was going to retire. He said, "Never! This is my life's work. I have to get this message to as many people as I can."

When you read How To Have A Great Day Everyday, you will realize, more than ever, that your life is all about the choices you make today. You choose. It's that simple. Read this book often. Practice the principles and watch your life change. And don't forget to share the book with others.

Thank you, Steve. You have given us all something that will truly last forever.

John P. Brandt, Jr.
Founder & President
The Brandt Group, Ltd.
Bozeman, Montana

Introduction

Hi, this is Steve Beck and this book will look at the topic of "How To Have A Great Day Everyday!"

I have made this book:

- Easy to read
- Easy to implement

We humans have a tendency to make our lives complicated. It doesn't have to be that way. Life is just not that complicated.

If you **don't** have A Great Day Everyday, do not discount the fact that it is possible for you; realize it's something to strive for, and that many people have A Great Day Everyday.

If you do have A Great Day Everyday...
Congratulations! I know it is not always easy to accomplish this, so keep it up because you are an inspiration for the rest of us.

The fact that you are reading this book right now:

indicates that the title has intrigued you,

or

you must have *some* interest in knowing how to have A Great Day Everyday,

or

someone recommended the book to you and you're wondering, "Why me? Do they think I need to read this book?" or…"Do they think something is wrong with me? Are they sending me a message?"

or

someone recommended the book to you and you are thinking, "How sweet they are to think of me."

Regardless of why you have this book in your hands, here's what I want you to do: Be open to the fact that it is possible for you to have A Great Day Everyday, and just go out into your world and do it!

Because our mood affects others, I feel we have the responsibility to learn how to Have a Great Day Everyday.

Here is who will be affected in a positive way by you having A Great Day Everyday.

- Parents
- Children
- Friends
- Spouse
- Sweetie pie
- Co-workers
- Customers
- Neighbors
- Anyone you encounter

I hope you enjoy this book and decide to make having A Great Day Everyday something you will work on for the rest of your life!

Love,

Steve Beck

"We have to do the best we can.
This is our sacred
human responsibility."

~ ALBERT EINSTEIN ~

"If you're not happy every morning when you get up and leave for work, you're not going to be successful."

~ **DONALD M. KENDALL** ~

Chapter One

WATCH YOUR THOUGHTS

Here is an exercise I recommend you practice starting right now and do it every day, several times throughout the course of the day, for the rest of your life.

Here's how it works: take your consciousness (your awareness) and place it about two feet above your head to the right or left.

This is how to do it: take your arm and put it straight in the air. Then bend your elbow and point your hand toward your head, pretending your hand is holding a small video camera watching you. Good! Now imagine this camera sees every move you make and every thought you have. Do it without judging your actions or thoughts. This practice of observing without judgment or noticing without judgment is called "witnessing."

By witnessing you'll notice:

- Your patterns of behavior
- Your addictions
- Your fears
- Your triggers
- Your manners
- Your anger
- Your past and how it affects you
- Your actions and the consequences they have on your friends, family, co-workers and strangers
- Your actions and the consequences they have on you
- How you eat
- How you walk
- How you drive
- How often your decisions are based upon your fears
- What frustrates you
- What excites you

Also look at your thoughts regarding:

- Other people (especially those not like you)
- Your body
- Your focus
- Your laziness
- Your competitiveness
- Your job
- Your romantic relationship or lack of one
- Your car
- Your home
- Traveling
- War
- Politics
- Money
- Sports

The only way to make changes in your life is to observe *how you do things and to change the things you think or feel will not support you in having A Great Day Everyday and to keep on doing the things that you KNOW will support you in having A Great Day Everyday.*

It is just that simple!

Also, notice your thoughts about the possibility of having A Great Day Everyday. In other words, when you first heard the idea of having A Great Day Everyday, did you think, "What? Are you crazy? Nobody can have A Great Day Everyday." Or did you think, "I know people who have A Great Day Everyday. I think it's possible. I don't, but I know people who do."

REMEMBER, THE THOUGHTS YOU HAVE ARE GOING TO DETERMINE YOUR SUCCESS IN HAVING A GREAT DAY EVERYDAY..... OR NOT.

"My mind is my biggest asset. I expect to win every tournament I play."

~ TIGER WOODS ~

Chapter Two

JUST CHOOSE TO

One way to have A Great Day Everyday is just to choose to. That's right! You just choose to have a great day first thing in the morning. Ed Forman, seminar leader, stated it best when he said, "When you get up in the morning, it's like you have a menu. You open up the menu and on the left side it says TERRIFIC and the right hand side it says TERRIBLE. You choose; it's just that simple."

Sometimes people say:
"I'm in a good mood on Fridays"
"I like paydays"
"I don't like Mondays"
"If only I had a different job"
"That stuff doesn't work for me"
"You should meet my wife"
"If I won the lottery, then…"
"I had a terrible childhood"

I say that you can have A Great Day Everyday and all you have to do is just choose to!

"Stop complaining about what you're not getting, and start creating what you want."

~ DR. PHIL MCGRAW ~

Chapter Three

LEAVE YOUR FUNK AT THE DOOR!

Another way to have A Great Day Everyday is to Leave Your Funk at the Door. This is what I have heard from a lot of people when they go to work.

They mumble:
"I don't know if I like this job."
"My manager is an idiot."
"Most of the people I work with are okay, but there are some real jerks I have to deal with."
"It's a long week and I don't know…"

My recommendation is that when you walk in the door at work, you say enthusiastically "Hey what's going on? FIRE UP EVERYONE! Let's do it; let's go! All right! Let's have a Great Day Today!"

And you'll become a powerful force where you work.

- For the company?
    Not necessarily, but they will benefit.
- For your co-workers?
    Not necessarily, but they will benefit.
- For the customers?
    Not necessarily, but they will benefit.

You do it for you because you are that kind of person.

Become the kind of person who is an addition and a positive energy force where you work. Don't wait for someone else to fire you up. You take charge! Become the kind of person people love to work with. This also applies when you come home at the end of the day. Let's say that you had a bad day or a rough day that day. You're walking in the door and you're mumbling when you walk in:

"I don't even know why I work there."

"My boss is an idiot."

"The people I work with...all they do is constantly complain and the customers are never happy."

I say, when you walk in that door at the end of the day and you shut that door, it sounds like this, "Hey what's going on? I'm home. Let's make some dinner? All right. Hey, let's do something great tonight!" And you become a positive energy force at home, too.

Do you know why? Because when you walk in at the end of the day, do you know what they want? They want you.

- **They don't want your funk.**
- **They don't want your junk.**
- **They don't want your terrible day.**

THEY WANT YOU!

"You can't teach what you don't know"

~ **STEVE BECK** ~

"There's only one corner of the universe you can be certain of improving, and that's your own self."

~ ALDOUS HUXLEY ~
AUTHOR OF
BRAVE NEW WORLD

Chapter Four

START WITH YOURSELF

Another way to have A Great Day Everyday is to start with yourself. In other words, don't worry about your mother. Don't worry about your father. Don't worry about your friends and neighbors. Watch out that you don't find yourself becoming jealous or nosy and saying, "She thinks that she is so cute," or "Who does he think he is?"

At work, accept the idea that people are doing the best they can and... don't hang out with people who are constantly negative. Have you ever heard yourself saying to a co-worker about another co-worker, "She's late everyday," or "He doesn't do half of the work I do."

Allow other people to just be. Focus on yourself. You work on you in this lifetime because you know what?...

**THIS AIN'T NO DRESS REHEARSAL.
THIS IS THE REAL THING, BABY!**

Check this out! The following words were written on the tomb of an Anglican Bishop in the crypts of Westminster Abby:

When I was young and free and my imagination had no limits, I dreamed of changing the world. As I grew older and wiser, I discovered that the world would not change so I shortened my sights somewhat and decided to change only my country. But it too seemed immovable. As I grew into my twilight years, in one last desperate attempt, I settled for changing only my family, those closest to me, but alas they would have none of it. And now, as I lay on my death bed, I suddenly realize if I only changed myself first, then, by example, I would have changed my family. From their inspiration and encouragement I would have been able to better my country and, who knows, I may have even changed the world.

(John H. Rhoades 1100 A.D.)

You see, if you want to change the world, you work on you. Start with yourself.

One way to begin to work on yourself is to implement some of the things mentioned in this book. One problem with our society is although people know what to do to make their life great, they don't do it and then they feel bad. Since they do not want anyone to notice, they point their finger at other people, society and politicians and become experts at criticizing everything and everyone.

Look at this saying I found along the way; it sure applies here:

THE EGO THINKS IT'S GOOD ENOUGH TO BE AN EXPERT INSTEAD OF DOING ANYTHING ABOUT WHAT IT KNOWS.

"To keep a lamp burning, we have to keep putting oil in it."

~ MOTHER TERESA ~

Chapter Five

APPRECIATE THE SMALL THINGS

Another way to have A Great Day Everyday is to appreciate the small things in your life, and sometimes it's the smallest things. Let me mention a few things you might want to look at and begin to appreciate. Blow them up and make them a big thing.

Here are a few:

- A hot shower
- Watching snow fall from your front room window
- Sending an e-mail or letter to a good friend that you haven't heard from in ages
- Taking a scenic drive on a beautiful day
- A chocolate milkshake
- A bubble bath
- A full moon
- Walking along the beach at sunrise
- A great meal
- Running through sprinklers
- A night out with great friends

- A crackling fire
- Playing with a new puppy
- A kiss
- Road trips with friends
- Swinging on a swing
- The smell of freshly baked chocolate chip cookies
- Snuggling up with a good book on a Sunday afternoon
- The anticipation just before someone opens up a present from you that you KNOW they are going to love
- Watching the sunset
- Riding your bike
- Getting out of bed every morning, being grateful for another beautiful day and realizing we have yet another day to create some wonderful and fabulous opportunities
- A good stretch
- Getting a hug from someone who cares deeply about you and that you care deeply about

"Today is a new day.
You will get out of
it just what you put into it."

~ MARY PICKFORD ~
ACADEMY AWARD WINNER
& CO-FOUNDER OF UNITED ARTISTS

Chapter Six

AFFIRM YOUR DAY

The next step in having A Great Day Everyday is the most powerful tool I have ever run into in my life. It is called affirming your day. Affirming your day has to do with looking in the mirror at the center part of your eye and saying positive things that directly relate to your life. Things like this:

- Today is a great day – I will be at my very best all day and all night long.
- I am very healthy and weigh _____(ideal weight.)
- I am focused, enthusiastic and organized.

Say these things when you are dressed and ready to go! Say them when you look your best. It is more believable that way.

When you begin to consistently affirm your day and look into the center part of your eye, your subconscious mind begins to believe what it's being told and acts upon those commands.

Your thoughts are like little puppies wanting your attention, and you can either walk around life like many people do being unfocused and going here, there, and everywhere, or... you can be the kind of person who is disciplined and has the life you want to have, the life you always knew that you could have.

How? By affirming your day with passion, excitement and enthusiasm.

Here are a few more affirmations you could use.

- I am radiantly beautiful, powerful, and joyous.
- Everything in my life is absolutely perfect just the way it is.
- Endless good now comes to me in endless ways.
- My good now flows to me in a steady, unbroken, ever increasing stream of success, happiness, and abundance.
- I give thanks for my permanent happiness, my permanent health, my permanent wealth, my permanent love.
- I talk always with confidence.
- I express myself fully and clearly at all times.
- Nothing is too good to be true. Nothing is too wonderful to happen. Nothing is too good to last.
- Today is a great day.

It's just that simple. You declaring TODAY IS A GREAT DAY. In other words, instead of the day playing you like an instrument, you're declaring that today is, in fact, A Great Day. Do it at the beginning of the day and then do it throughout the course of the day. Do it until you begin to believe it. Once you believe it, you will begin to see it manifest in your life and become reality.

What happens with us is that we are waiting for success to walk through the door and jump into our laps. Hey, I'll tell ya', it is not going to happen.

If you want success to happen in your life, you have to create it. The way to do it is through affirmations. Talk to yourself in a positive way. It is called positive self-talk. By talking to yourself in a positive way, you will see miracles happen in your life!

Here's another one.

- I feel happy, healthy and terrific.

In America, we live in the wealthiest society on the planet and we are the most depressed. How come? Because we are not taking responsibility for our lives.

You have to begin to take responsibility for your life to make your life great.

NOBODY ELSE WILL MAKE YOUR LIFE GREAT. IT IS UP TO YOU.

Let me just talk about affirming your day and the results it can create. I did a seminar for a large computer company where an account manager named Peter was a participant. A few months after the seminar he exclaimed to me, "Steve, I was in your sales training last February. I have been saying in the mirror everyday, 'I am an excellent sales person and my customers love doing business with me.' I have been saying, 'I am having my best quarter.' Peter then told me that the previous quarter was the best quarter he had ever had! He said if it were not for affirming his day every day, it would not have happened.

I hear this all the time from sales people who have record quarters and record years because they are affirming their day. *This exercise is essential for your success in having A Great Day Everyday.*

I have had mothers and fathers tell me they have better relationships with their kids. Affirming your day has to do with you creating better health in your life. Affirming your day has to do with you creating and manifesting what it is you want in your life.

Here is a question for you. *What do you want?* Most people want to be happy, satisfied and know their life makes a difference. You can get there by affirming your day. Happiness and satisfaction are by-products of you working very hard towards achieving what it is you want in your life, towards worthwhile goals. I highly recommend that you have goals. Write down your short term goals, (six months to one year), your intermediate goals (3-5 years) and your long term goals (10 years).

Most people do not get what they want in their life because they don't ask. Setting personal and professional goals is a road map for your success in having A Great Day Everyday.

"And life is what we
make it.
Always has been, always
will be."

~ GRANDMA MOSES ~

Chapter Seven

FOCUS ON THE POSITIVE

Another way to have A Great Day Everyday is to focus on the positive. Rather than focusing on your limitations, focus on your opportunities and possibilities. There are plenty out there for all of us. And stop worrying. I heard a statistic that said 70% of the things we worry about never happened or will never happen to us. How crazy is that? It's like we create things and imagine situations that will most likely never happen. Then we worry about them. It does not make any sense.

ENJOY YOUR LIFE!!!

HERE IS A LITTLE STORY THAT RELATES!

A Tale of Two Men...

Two men, both seriously ill, occupied the same hospital room. One man was allowed to sit up in his bed for an hour each afternoon to help drain the fluid from his lungs. His bed was next to the room's only window. The other man had to spend all his time flat on his back. The men talked for hours on end. They spoke of their wives and families, their homes, their jobs, their involvement in the military service, even where they had been on vacation.

Every afternoon when the man in the bed by the window could sit up, he would pass the time by describing to his roommate all the things he could see outside the window. The man in the other bed began to live for those one-hour periods where his world would be broadened and enlivened by all the activity and color of the world outside. The window overlooked a park with a lovely lake.

Ducks and swans played on the water while children sailed their model boats. Young lovers walked arm in arm amidst flowers of every color. Grand old trees graced the landscape, and a fine view of the city skyline could be seen in the distance.

As the man by the window described all this in exquisite detail, the man on the other side of the room would close his eyes and imagine the picturesque scene. One warm afternoon the man by the window described a parade passing by. Although the other man couldn't hear the band, he could see it in his mind's eye as the gentleman by the window portrayed it with descriptive words. Days and weeks passed in similar fashion.

One morning, the day nurse arrived to bring water for their baths only to find the lifeless body of the man by the window, who had died peacefully in his sleep. She was saddened and called the hospital attendants to take the body away. As soon as it seemed appropriate, the other man asked if he could be moved next to the window. The nurse was happy to make the switch, and after making sure he was comfortable, she left him alone.

Slowly, painfully, he propped himself up on one elbow to take his first look at the world outside. Finally, he would have the joy of seeing it for himself. He strained to slowly turn to look out the window beside the bed. It faced a bare wall. The man asked the nurse what could have compelled his deceased roommate to describe such wonderful things outside this window. The nurse responded that the man was blind and could not even see the wall. She said, "Perhaps he just wanted to encourage you."

Epilogue...There is tremendous happiness in making others happy, despite our own situations. Shared grief is half the sorrow, but shared happiness is doubled. If you want to feel rich, just count all of the things you have that money can't buy.

"I want to be thoroughly used up when I die, for the harder I work the more I live."

~ GEORGE BERNARD SHAW ~

Chapter Eight

RECOGNIZE YOUR GIFT

Another way to have A Great Day Everyday is to recognize that you have been given a gift. This gift is called **Your Life on the Planet Earth**. Did you know that scientists have said our body is worth 500 million to a billion dollars? Can you imagine that? Here you are walking around with a billion dollar machine called your body. You gotta love that. Once you recognize your body is a gift, then you will begin to appreciate your body and appreciate the gift you have been given. When you do recognize that you have been given this great gift, you will say, "Thank You" often.

"Let no one ever come to you without leaving better and happier. Be the living expression of kindness: kindness in your face, kindness in your eyes, kindness in your smile, kindness in your warm greeting."

~ MOTHER TERESA ~

Chapter Nine

STRIVE TO DO YOUR BEST

Another way to have A Great Day Everyday is always strive to do your best. Get up in the morning, look in the mirror and say, *"Today is a Great Day. I will be at my very best all day and all night long."* Be the best in everything you do whether you are a:

- Father
- Mother
- CEO
- Nurse
- Accountant
- Customer service representative
- Bank teller
- Doctor

- Construction worker
- Administrative assistant
- Manager
- Supervisor
- Student
- Lawyer
- Real estate agent
- Sales representative
- Police officer
- Financial advisor
- Pilot

It does not matter what you do. What DOES matter is HOW you do what you do; so do your best, not for anyone else, but for yourself. Everyone wants to be happy and satisfied. *You will find happiness and satisfaction by doing your best every single day.*

"To the attentive eye, each moment of the year has its own beauty."

~ RALPH WALDO EMERSON ~

Chapter Ten

BLESSED

Another way to have A Great Day Everyday is to appreciate your life.

You see we are blessed, yet sometimes we do not see or remember how blessed we are. If you can get in touch with your appreciation of how much you have and how blessed you really are and then share that with others in your world, you will then find your happiness, and you will be satisfied.

What follows are some thought provoking statements by Robert Nolan. I recommend you make a really nice copy of this, frame it, and hang it on the wall.

Let this serve as a gentle reminder of how precious life is.

If you woke up this morning with more health than illness, you are more blessed than the million people who will not survive the week.

If you never experience the danger of battle, the loneliness of imprisonment, the agony of torture, or the pains of starvation, you are ahead of 500 million people around the world.

If you attend a church meeting without fear of harassment, arrest, or death, you are more blessed than almost 3 billion people in the world.

If you have food in your refrigerator, clothes on your back, a roof over your head, and place to sleep, you are richer than 75% of this world.

If you have money in the bank, in your wallet, and spare change in a dish someplace, you are among the top 8% of the world's wealthy.

If you hold up your head with a smile on your face and are truly thankful, you are blessed because the majority can but most do not.

If you can read this message, then you are more blessed than over 2 billion people in the world that cannot read anything at all.[1]

---

1   Robert Nolan, www.randomania.net

"Learn to enjoy every minute of your life. Be happy now. Don't wait for something outside of yourself to make you happy in the future. Think how really precious is the time you have to spend, whether it's at work or with your family. Every minute should be enjoyed and savored."

~ EARL NIGHTINGALE ~

Chapter Eleven

DO SOMETHING EACH DAY

Another way to have A Great Day Everyday is to do something each day to improve your:

- Physical health
- Mental health
- Spiritual health

When I was in sixth grade I had a nun who said, **"Good, Better, Best, never let it rest. May the good be better and the better best."** It drove me crazy at the time because she said it so often, but I never forgot it.

Here are a couple of tips to improve your physical health.

- Walk for a half hour each day
- Swim for twenty minutes three times a week
- Ride your bike for twenty minutes to an hour
- Eat more salads than red meat
- Drink plenty of water

Here are a couple of tips to improve your mental health.

- Affirm your day
- Talk to yourself in a positive way
- See the positive side of things instead of the negative side of things
- Watch less news on television

Here are a couple of tips to improve your spiritual health.

- Pray; Pray for yourself; Pray for other people
- Meditate. Take twenty or thirty minutes each day and just focus on your breathing. The recommended time to do this is between 3 a.m. and 6 a.m.

When I first heard this information about how to have a great life, I was 27 years old at a motivational weekend seminar. I was in the back of the room and I will never forget the speaker talking about Having A Great Life, You Can Do It! And I thought, "Oh, stop it. You don't know me. You have no idea what my life is like. I don't like Mondays, and... I don't like cloudy days. In fact, when it's cloudy for a couple of days, I'm in a little bit of a funk. When it's cloudy for about a week straight, I get a little depressed. I'm intimidated by beautiful women. I'm intimidated by men who have it more together than I do." Then all of the sudden I had a painful realization.

I heard in my head...."You're a wimp. You're controlled by the day of the week. You're controlled by the weather. You're controlled by other people. You're a wimp!" I didn't like what I heard, but it was true. I thought, "It is true; I am a wimp."

And I vowed right then for the rest of my life to have A Great Day Everyday. Has it happened? No. Does it happen the majority of the time? Yes.

IT'S SOMETHING TO STRIVE FOR.

"We will relentlessly pursue perfection. Even though achieving perfection is impossible, we will chase it anyway. In the process we will attain excellence."

~ VINCE LOMBARDI ~

Chapter Twelve

HAVE POSITIVE THOUGHTS

Another way to have A Great Day Everyday is to think positive thoughts.

Let me ask you a couple of questions:

If you planted watermelon seeds in the ground, what do you think that you would get? That's right. Watermelons!
If you planted onions seeds in the ground, what do you think you would get? That's right. Onions!
If you planted potato seeds in the ground, what are you going to get? Correct again! Potatoes!

And if you plant negative thoughts in your head, what do you think you are going to get? You are going to have negative experiences which add up to a negative life. That is why it is so important to have positive thoughts about yourself, about other people, and about the world you live in.

Now, if you want to have negative thoughts, watch the news, and read the newspaper everyday, (especially the front page), then you will be convinced we live in a terrible place and life is not really worth living. **It is up to you to put in those positive thoughts every single day!**

It's called the *Law of Attraction*, and the law of attraction states, "Whatever you think about the most will be attracted to you."

IT'S A SIMPLE CONCEPT.

Have you ever worked with or known people who are truly negative? They keep saying how lucky some people are, but not them. They talk about people getting breaks in life, but not them.

When something positive is talked about, they are the first ones to say it won't last or it was a fluke. They consistently point out that life is difficult, unfair, and that people shouldn't be trusted.

They talk about negative things that keep happening in their lives. Why? Because it's true. Negative things keep happening to them, because they are attracting negative things by their negative thoughts.

Have you ever been around positive people? They have fun and play with life as if it were a game. Isn't it true that they seemingly create positive things in their lives? If you have positive thoughts about people, positive thoughts about yourself, and positive thoughts about your world, you are going to have a positive experience. It's called the Law of Attraction.

"*I will smile at friend and foe alike and make every effort to find, in him or her, a quality to praise, now that I realize the deepest yearning of human nature is the craving to be appreciated.*"

~ OG MANDINO ~

Chapter Thirteen

PRACTICE THE AFL METHOD

The next way to have A Great Day Everyday is to practice the AFL method. AFL stands for:

- **A**ccept
- **F**orgive
- **L**ove

This has to do with people who are not like you, and do not live life like you. They have a different mind set. They are a different color than you. Most of the time you do not understand why they live life in a way that does not make sense to you. Here is the way to deal with that situation. You just **A**ccept them, (not necessarily agree with them), just accept that that's the way they are.

If people are different from you and they have a different culture, they talk different, or they look different, just accept them for the way they are and then Forgive yourself for that instantaneous judgement call that we all make. Get to the point of Loving them for the way they are and the way they are not.

It is called the AFL method.

- Accept
- Forgive
- Love

"Too often we underestimate the power of a touch, a smile, a kind word, a listening ear, an honest compliment, or the smallest act of caring, all of which have the potential to turn a life around."

~ LEO BUSCAGLIA ~

Chapter Fourteen

LIVE IN THE PRESENT MOMENT

Another way to have A Great Day Everyday is to live in the present moment, which really means to let go of your past. There is nothing you can do about your past -- it is already gone. The future? You want to worry about that? Prepare, yes! Worry, No! It might never come! So look at today as THE DAY. Look at this moment as a perfect moment because there are so many opportunities here. Be focused, organized, and you will see that you will be much more productive and, as a result, you will be happier because you're not worrying so much.

Why is this important? Worry causes stress and stress affects your health in a negative way. That is not good. Stop at least once a day, look around and begin to appreciate your life. Discover the good in your life and appreciate what you have been given at a super deep level. When you do this, you will see magic and experience miracles in your life.

People who have A Great Day Everyday:

- Appreciate Mondays
- Achieve their professional and personal goals
- Push themselves
- Smile a lot
- Have a great appreciation of nature
- Have a great appreciation of other people
- Have fun with their life
- Laugh
- Accept the hand they've been dealt
- Take care of their health
- Love people and love life
- Have a sense of adventure and take risks

"You have powers you never dreamed of. You can do things you never thought you could do. There are no limitations in what you can do except the limitations of your own mind."

~ **DARWIN P. KINGSLEY** ~

Chapter Fifteen

PROGRAMMING

Another way to have A Great Day Everyday is to realize you have been programmed to think you are not O.K. How could this have happened?

Let's investigate this. Do you know how many commercials a child will see in one year? Think about it. The number of commercials a child sees in one year is 30,000, which means that 30,000 times a year kids hear "You'd be fine if you had our product."

The statistics say that 95-100 percent of the time kids are watching TV, they are being told (through commercials) they are not okay the way they are. Here is the deal. Did you watch TV when you were a kid? Do you still watch TV? If you don't feel good about yourself it might be conditioning. It might be programming. It does not have to be this way. That is why affirming your day is so important to get you out of that funk, junk and gunk that is the lie that says you are not O.K.

You are, in fact, GREAT just the way you are.

You are PERFECT just the way you are.

You are EXCELLENT just the way you are.

You see, it is up to you to **reprogram the program** so you can take back your personal power that has been taken from you and begin to, or continue to, have A Great Day Everyday.

"Success is not going to walk
through the door and jump onto
your lap and lick your face
like a puppy.
YOU have to create your
success every day."

~ STEVE BECK ~

"It always amazes me how some people who are born with so little accomplish so much, and how others who are born with so much accomplish so little."

~ LOU HOLTZ ~

Chapter Sixteen

YOU ARE IN CHARGE OF YOUR LIFE

Another way to have A Great Day Everyday is to recognize you are in charge of your life and this is what I mean. YOU have emotions. YOU have a body. YOU have a day of the week. YOU have thoughts. YOU have feelings. YOU have desires. Let me make it easy.

Look at this chart.

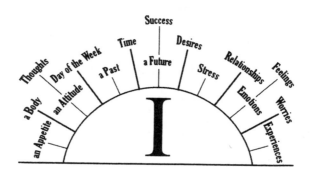

Once you recognize that you are the I in this chart, and YOU are in charge of these things in your life, then you will be free. By not taking charge of these elements on the chart, you automatically put those elements in charge. You become irresponsible. You give away your personal power and you become a victim of your own life.

Let's look at a few of these:
Day of the Week. Are you the kind of person who hates Mondays? If that is the case, then Mondays won't be so friendly to you. That means 1/7th of your life, you will be angry and maybe even depressed because it is Monday.

How about your past? Does your past rule you, or do you rule your past?

How about stress? Is stress in charge of your life, or are YOU in charge of your stress? And I'll tell you why I ask this. Do you know when people have the most heart attacks in our western society? The day of the week and the time when people have the most heart attacks in our society is Monday mornings at 9 o'clock. So I must ask again...

Are you in charge of your stress, or is your stress in charge of you?

Are you in charge of your appetite, or is your appetite in charge of you?

Are you in charge of your feelings, or are your feelings in charge of you?

Are you in charge of your thoughts, or are your thoughts in charge of you?

How life works is you have thoughts, and thoughts create your point of view and your point of view then determines your actions. So if we go backwards -- your actions are determined by your point of view; your point of view comes from your thoughts.

So...

- What are your thoughts about you?
- What are your thoughts about this life that you have?
- What are your thoughts about your job?
- What are your thoughts about your relationship or lack of one?
- What are your thoughts about your emotions?
- What are your thoughts about your fears?

Once you begin to take charge of these things in your life, you will have A Great Day Everyday.

Why? It is because people *want* to have A Great Day Everyday. It's a natural thing to want to "Have A Great Day Every Single Day."

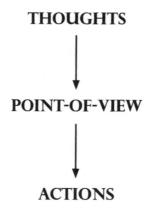

THOUGHTS

↓

POINT-OF-VIEW

↓

ACTIONS

Here are a few questions that you must ask yourself:

- Am I a warrior or a worrier?
- Am I a winner or a whiner?
- Am I high maintenance or low maintenance?
- Am I part of the problem or part of the solution?

*"Life is not happening to You,
you are directing the life that
is flowing through you."*

~ REV. MICHAEL SPEER ~

"*You have brains in your head.*
You have feet in your shoes.
You can steer yourself any
direction you choose."

~ DR. SEUSS ~
OH, THE PLACES YOU'LL GO!

Chapter Seventeen

YOUR LIFE AS A PLAY

The next step in having A Great Day Everyday is realizing it is about attitude. When I heard "Attitude is Everything!" for the hundredth time, I thought, "Awww come on. I'm sick of hearing that expression!" I didn't like it anymore. It did not do anything for me.

Let's look at it from a different perspective. Let's look at attitude from a completely different point of view. Let's look at your life as a book being written or, let's say, A PLAY. Let's look at your life as if you are involved in a play. You are the writer, you are the director, and you are the star of your play.

So, if that is the case, how are you going to be later on today or tonight? How are you going to be tomorrow? How about the next day? And this coming weekend and next month and next year?

If you are in the middle of a play and you are the writer, how are you going to write your script?

If you are negative, you say, "I don't know... probably with a negative twist, in which case I end up depressed like always!"

I am saying this. How would you like to be? How do you want to be later today or tonight? How do you want to be tomorrow? And the next day? And this coming weekend? And next month and next year...?

Tomorrow, you can be whatever and however you want to be. **Tomorrow's page is blank!** That page of your life is blank because it has not been lived yet. How would you like to be tomorrow? How about the day after tomorrow? And what about the day after that? See your life as a play, where you are the writer, director, and star of your own play.

So once again...How do you want your life to be? You can have it any way you want it. YOU are in charge of your life!

"If you're not playing a big
enough game, you'll screw up
the game you're playing just to
give yourself something to do."

~ **ANONYMOUS** ~

*"In the middle of
difficulty
lies opportunity."*

~ ALBERT EINSTEIN ~

"People are like
stained-glass windows.
They sparkle when the sun is out,
but when the darkness sets in,
their true beauty is revealed only
if there is a light from within."

~ **ELISABETH KUBLER-ROSS** ~

Chapter Eighteen

YOU WON A GAME

The next step to having A Great Day Everyday is pretending that you have won a game. Let's go back to about nine months to a year before you were born, and you were living on, let's say, Mars. Have you ever seen some of the pictures from Mars? Mars is cold and stark. There is not even any water on Mars. So... let's say you are on Mars and somebody pulls out this ticket and says, "Hey you won".

And you say, "What? What did I win?"

He replies, "Life on earth."

And you say, "Oh my gosh, am I like an alligator, or a lizard, or a frog?"

And he says, "Noooooooo."

And you shout, "Oh my gosh, I'm a pet. I'm somebody's pet. I can live in someone's house, be warm in the winter, and they will feed me and pet me."

And he replies, "Nooooooo. You won First Prize. You get to be a human being."

And you are ecstatic and say, "Oh no, you're kidding me! You mean I get to go to earth and have kids, get a job, drive a car, make money, and eat chocolate cake?"

And he says, "Yea, You won first prize and it's called 'Life on the Planet Earth'.

Here you are. You made it!

CONGRATULATIONS!

"Time is limited, so I better wake up every morning fresh and know that I have just one chance to live this particular day right, and to string my days together into a life of action and purpose."

~ LANCE ARMSTRONG ~

Chapter Nineteen

HEAVEN

Another way to have A Great Day Everyday is imagining this is heaven. Here's how this works. Can you imagine dying and going up to the pearly gates? There's this huge guy wearing white robes and he has a name tag that says Michael.

So you say, "Hey, Michael? What's up, baby? I'm through with that crap they call life on the planet Earth. Now, which way is Heaven man? Which way's Heaven -- down this hall or that hall? What's the deal?"

And Michael slowly turns toward you with his eyes lowered, looking almost sorry for you and says, "Ohhh... you didn't get it?"

And you ask, "Get what? Get What? What are you talkin' about? What's the deal? Come on, man which way is Heaven?"

And Michael hesitates and very slowly and remorsefully says, "You…. you must not have gotten it."

And you say rather quickly and impatiently, "What are you talking about? Which way is Heaven? This way or that way?"

He says, "Heaven huh?"

You exclaim, "Yeah, yeah, yeah, yeah, yeah, yeah!"

And Michael looks right into the center of your eyes and says, "You were just there."

Hey, can you imagine what you are in the middle of, is Heaven? Can you imagine finding out when you are all done that this is Heaven? What a huge mistake that would be. What a huge problem that would be.

Let me ask you a few questions:

- Do you think there are ice cream cones in Heaven?
- Do you think there are rainbows in Heaven?
- Do you think there are little girls with huge brown eyes wearing beautiful dresses and little boys in their suits and ties in Heaven?
- Do you think there are steaks and salads and great food like we eat in Heaven?
- Do you think there is beautiful blue water and blue skies and clouds in Heaven?

I'll tell you something. You ought to look again at where you live… because...

THIS MIGHT JUST BE HEAVEN!

"The sun is always shining. Even though clouds may come along and obscure the sun for a while, the sun is always shining. The sun never stops shining. And even though the earth turns, and the sun appears to go down, it really never stops shining."

~ LOUISE L. HAY ~

"I know what I'm gonna do tomorrow and the next day and the next year and the year after that."

**~ GEORGE BAILEY ~
IN
. IT'S A WONDERFUL LIFE**

Chapter Twenty

SPREAD THE WORD

We want three things in our lives. We want to:

1. Be happy
2. Be satisfied
3. Know our life has made a difference

One way you make a difference is by spreading the concept of having A Great Day Everyday with your friends and family. If they spread the word with their loved ones, who then spread the word with their loved ones, who then go and share this concept with their friends and families, and it goes on and on and on, then maybe we won't have the negativity, the anger, the frustration, the criticism that we all deal with every day, and maybe, just maybe, we will live in peace having A Great Day Everyday!

You will make a difference by creating your own ripple effect.

It is your choice! Please make a conscious choice to become part of the solution rather than part of the problem.

The following is one of my favorite sayings. I read it at the end of my Customer Service Seminars. I have heard that a copy hung over Mother Teresa's bed. It's called ANYWAY.

ANYWAY

People are often illogical,
unreasonable and self-centered.
Love them anyway.

If you do good,
people will accuse you of selfish, ulterior motives.
Do good anyway.

If you are successful, you will win
false friends and true enemies.
Succeed anyway.

The good you do today will be forgotten tomorrow.
Do good anyway.

Honesty and frankness make you vulnerable.
Be honest and frank anyway.

The biggest men and women with the biggest
ideas can be shot down by the smallest men
and women with the smallest minds.
Think big anyway.

People favor underdogs but follow only top dogs.
Fight for a few underdogs anyway.

What you spend years building may be
destroyed overnight.
Build anyway.

People really need help but may
attack you if you do help them.
Help people anyway.

Give the world the best you have and
you'll get kicked in the teeth.
Give the world the best you have anyway.[2]

---

2   With permission from the author, Kent M. Keith, © 1968,
renewed 2001, The Paradoxical Commandments

"The life of the individual only has meaning insofar as it aids in making the life of every living thing nobler and more beautiful."

~ **ALBERT EINSTEIN** ~

Appendix A: Recommended Reading

<u>A New Earth</u> by Eckhart Tolle. Penguin Group 2005.

<u>The Power of Now: A Guide to Spiritual Enlightenment</u> by Eckhart Tolle. New World Library 1999.

<u>The Secret</u> by Rhonda Byrne. Simon & Schuster 2006.

<u>Focal Point: A Proven System to Simplify Your Life, Double Your Productivity, and Achieve All Your Goals</u> by Brian Tracy. American Management Association 2001.

<u>The Four Agreements</u> by Don Miguel Ruiz. Amber-Allen Publishing,Inc. 1997.

<u>What to Say When You Talk to Yourself</u> by Shad Helmstetter. Pocket Books 1997.

<u>Creative Visualization: Use the Power of Your Imagination to Create What You Want In Your Life</u> by Shakti Gawain. Nataraj Publishing 1978.

<u>The Science of Getting Rich</u> by Wallace Wattles. Online, www.wallacewattles.com.

Seminars and Keynote Speeches by Steve Beck

The E.C.S. (X) Factor (Part I, II, & III)
- Delivering Exceptional Customer Service

The E.C.S. (X) Factor Sales Training
- How to increase sales & decrease stress

Goal Setting
- Preparing for your future today

Leadership
- What it takes to be a great leader

Time Management
- Fitting a 10-hour day into 8

Communication Skills
- Being part of the solution

Stress Management
- Learning how to get it done with ease

Coaching
- The art of encouragement

Effective Presentation Skills
- Getting through fear to accomplish greatness

How to Have a Great Day Everyday CD.
To order visit www.beckseminars.com

Thank you for reading this book. Let's all join together in sharing the concept of having A Great Day Everyday with people we love.

It starts with you. If you are waiting for someone else to begin, guess what? They're probably waiting for you.

The time is now! And remember to have fun doing it!

Looking forward to seeing you along the path...

Sincerely,
Steve Beck